PRINTERS TALES

Compiled By:
David Hughes

ISBN: 1495377482
ISBN-13: 978-1495377488

Body Text: Gandhi Serif
Headings: League Gothic

Contents

Introduction

PRINTERS' TALES is a compilation of over 30 stories, from various authors, about the printing industry in the pre-digital age.

Before computers became common-place in the late 1970s, to produce a printed page required the skill and expertise of a multitude of time-served craftsmen.

Compositors worked with lead type to create words letter by letter. Paper was pressed on to inked letters to reproduce words and sentences.

Many of these skills have long-since been forgotten. This compilation brings together memories of the printing and newspaper industries from that era.

Many stories involve the Linotype machine, a mechanical typesetting machine, that was used to produce newspapers, and other publications, from the 1880s until the computer revolution of the 1970s/80s.

There are stories, poems and limericks from authors from the USA, Canada, UK, Australia and New Zealand, all of whom share a common workplace experience.

From tales from American "tramp printers" who were able to travel the length and breadth of the United States working on various newspapers on the way, to the unique language and terminology used by compositors on a London Fleet Street "companionship" and lots of stories in between.

Local Newspaper Memories

by Dave Hughes

I WAS first introduced to the Linotype machine in the mid 1970s when I started work as an Apprentice Compositor at the Yorkshire Evening Press, then located in Coney Street, York.

The rear of the premises overlooked the River Ouse in the city centre. Although the site was redeveloped some time ago, the building can still be identified by the Yorkshire Herald sign (in stone) that was left intact.

There were over 20 machines in the room including some then state-of-the-art Intertype Monarchs. These machines had the keyboard blanked off and ran from punched tape which was produced in an adjacent room.

Producing the tape for the Tele-typesetting, as the process was called, was a 2-stage process. Firstly a tape was produced by an operator using a Qwerty keyboard with no reference to line-ends, justification, etc. This tape was then passed through a huge computer which worked out the line-lengths, justification, hyphenation, etc. and produced a second tape to be used on the Monarchs.

There were 8 Monarchs, in two rows of 4, with one man monitoring them all. He had to keep an eye on the slugs coming out of the machines to make sure they didn't spill off the end of the galley, keep the machines supplied with lead ingots (or pigs) and put a new tape on a machine when it had finished the previous job.

These machines were the real sports cars of the Linotype world, built for speed, with Perspex magazines bearing a gold crown logo. The bulk of the features section of the newspaper was produced on these machines because the copy was received well in advance. It was approximately two years before I actually got to operate a Linotype. This was a very satisfying experience, but always offset with a little tension. The combination of a slack line and a badly maintained machine could cause a 'splash' where molten lead was sprayed from the machine. It was not uncommon for operators to have to visit the local hospital casualty department for treatment for the burns sustained.

The machines at the Yorkshire Evening Press ranged from the nearly-new Intertype Monarchs, to some big machines with extra side magazines used in the display advertising department which I would guess dated back to the 1920s. I understand that there was a machine called a Linotype Elektron which was similar to the Intertype Monarch but I never came across one.

I remember on my first visit to the Science Museum in London seeing the Linotype machine they had there, I think it was a Model 65. Compared to a lot of the machines in daily use at the Yorkshire Evening Press it was very modern!

After finishing my apprenticeship I got itchy feet and decided to move to London. I worked at the South London Press from 1980-1989.

During the 1980s the typesetters union, the National Graphical Association (NGA), was facing some serious challenges from the Conservative Thatcher government. The first person to really test the newly-introduced anti-union laws was Eddie Shah at his Stockport Messenger plant. A handful of people were sacked for joining the NGA and then asking to be paid the agreed union minimum rate (effectively sacked for joining a union). I was a regular on the picket line there. The violence gradually escalated, seemingly in proportion to the number of police deployed. This culminated in an horrific night of violence with unmarked police from Merseyside and mounted police being deployed to beat the pickets into submission.

Eddie Shah paved the way for Rupert Murdoch to set up his "Fortress Wapping" plant in London's Docklands. This started the exodus of newspapers from London's Fleet Street area.

Each printing plant re-location resulted in the loss of many jobs previously carried out by print union members. The latest technology meant that journalists were able to key in and format their own stories. Even people selling advertising space were able to key in classified advertising while taking the copy over the phone.

The Linecaster
By Mike Wilson

In far-off days,
when Macintosh deterred the rain,
and hot metal reigned supreme,
there dwelt abroad,
in solitary splendour or ranked and rowed:
the linecaster.

Sired by Heath Robinson
out of necessity's invention,
this mechanism of complications
stands proud in print shops throughout the land.

Nimble fingers of willing acolytes
caress its keys,
and matrices,
those elegant stars of brassed precision,
fall into lines
to greet the molten lead.

Solidified then kissed by ink
the type speeds news and information
to the masses,
waging war on ignorance.

They are gone,
and words have lost a meaning –
casting, matrix, elevator, liner, vice –
or have been lost – disser, star-wheel, quadder;
our language is bereft.

What now the linecaster?

Memories, and museum piece;
still, noble men with cherished skills,
give reverence to freedom's friend:

The Linotype.

Canadian Typeset

by Roy Daniels

EMIGRATING to Canada in May of 1949 on the Cunard Ship Acquitania at the age of 12 was a harrowing experience. The lovely spring of England was replaced by the snow covered hills of Sudbury, Ontario.

It is a mining and smelting community that once produced 98 per cent of the world's nickel.

The smelting process produced clouds of sulphur dioxide that stripped the hills of their remaining foliage.

Three years later I became an apprentice at the Sudbury Daily Star. The paper was quite small and had a circulation of some 45,000.

For the first 18 months of my trade I performed the duties of a printer's devil. Picking up type and proofing it, mixing ink for the proof press, killing pages, sorting spacing and correcting galleys.

Learning to mirror-read type became as easy as the conventional way. In the ensuing years the journeymen made sure I knew all aspects of the trade.

I became well versed in the operation of linotype, intertype, ludlow and elrod.

When the teletypesetters came in the union printers had typing instructors come in and teach us how to type. At first it was the slower justified tape punching but with the coming of computers we switched to unjustified.

Leaving Sudbury in 1968 I travelled north to a little town on the shores of Lake Temiskaming called New Liskeard. My new wife (Carmen) and I lived there for

18 months before being called back to Sudbury to work as foreman at Journal Printing, a small job shop.

The call of newspaper printing was strong and when the Star called me I returned there. On a trip to southern Ontario, I chanced to visit the Kitchener Waterloo Record and talked to the production manager.

He asked me to fill out an application form and within hours I was hired away from the Star. Within a year the Record made plans to move to a new plant and in 1972 moved all the linotypes and with a new Goss letterpress started printing from the new location.

Within 5 years the linotypes were replaced and "cold type" came in. Adaption came easily and soon the production department changed to cut and paste. The press plates changed from lead to Napp aluminium.

In 1992, when the acquisition of newspapers seemed to peak, the Record was finally acquired by Torstar, producers of the Toronto Star. Our pressroom was closed and our pressmen were offered work at the giant Vaughn press plant.

Some took advantage of this, some retired and some made the transition to production work.

Adapting again, I started working in the scanning department scanning for ads, obits and celebrations.

At the same time, we started sending our completed pages electronically to Vaughn, so I became quite proficient in this department.

The Record, in trying to bring in new people offered buyouts to the older printers. Some of us accepted. I retired in 1998 at the age of 60 but was asked to come back on a part-time basis.

I am still working there three days a week and more when they are short handed.

It has been a rewarding trade. I met and enjoyed the company of many great and skilled journeymen printers from all over the world.

I have been a member of ITU and the Guild. Also a local union in Kitchener. I don't get a chance to set type any more, but the memories of hot type are still with me.

A Glossary of Printing Trade Terms

by George Clark

A Chapel.-A meeting of compositors is called a chapel, and the members of the chapel form a companionship (shortened to 'ship) pledged to watch over the interests of the London Society of Compositors (L.S.C.) and its members in the chapel.

A Wrong Fount.-A wrong fount is a letter of a different fount found among the correct fount. A shady kind of fellow is also referred to as a "wrong fount".

An "Out".-When a compositor accidentally omits a word or a phrase it is termed an "out", and if several words are missing the reader writes in the margin of the proof "Out-See copy", and pins the copy to the proof for return to the compositor for correction.

Bridging.-A compositor is said to have "bridged" if he fails to appear at the appointed time to put the line on, and forwards no reason for his absence.

Chopper.-A companion is choppery when he is surly and unapproachable and therefore looks hatchet faced: hence having a chopper on.

Clerk of the Chapel.-A member elected to act as secretary at meetings, take and read minutes, collect subscriptions and dues, prepare Chapel sheets, pay Chapel money into the Society, and give each quarter a proper account of Chapel events. The Father and the Clerk are the only responsible officials recognised by the Society on the Chapel's behalf.

Cocking a Deaf 'Un.-Pretending not to hear something particularly addressed to oneself.

Cutting the "Line".-When a mealtime break is due, the Father of the Chapel calls, "Cut the line, gentlemen", and each compositor stops work, resuming when the Father calls "Line on, gentlemen". All piece hands must have an equal chance of the work provided, and in this manner it is ensured. The copy provided by the Printer is lifted according to the Chapel rota. When the last page is sent into the foundry the Father "cuts the line", and announces the number of men required to stop for the next edition; the others go home.

Earwigging.-Listening to conversation that is intended to be private.

Fat.-Work easy of performance at adequate rates.

Father of the Chapel.-A compositor elected by his fellows to see that the customs of the trade, scales, conditions of work, etc., are strictly followed, and disputes avoided. No other member of the Chapel is allowed to interview the Printer or management unless accompanied by the Father.

Front Pages, Back Pages, and Side Pages.-Where two compositors are working side by side they are known as side pages; where three are working, the one in the middle refers to his companions as "my right-hand side page" and "my left-hand side page"; if the men are working back to back they are known as back pages; if frames or machines are-set facing each other, the men are front pages.

G.H.-Is an expression which means that the one who uses it is indicating to another that the one treating of a subject under discussion should go home and teach his grandmother to suck eggs. When a piece of stale news is related the cry goes round, "G.H.!"

K.D.-The meaning of K.D. is to keep anything dark; that is, not to relate it outside the present company.

Knowing Your Boxes.-Being aware of what you are doing or talking about. One of the first things an apprentice compositor is taught is the layout of the upper and lower cases, which means the geography of the types contained in them.

Machine Compositor.-Is a compositor with the added knowledge of the Linotype, Intertype, Monotype, Ludlow, etc. He is usually called an Operator.

Miles's Boy.-Miles was a printer in the old days, whose apprentice was knowing and artful: to whom all sorts of news came. Hence "According to Miles's Boy".

Nailing.-To nail is to talk derogatively (usually in a quiet fashion) of another compositor. The Nailbox is a traditionally mythical box full of' nails, long and short, which are said to be driven into a person who is absent.

N.F.-A fish rises to a fly as bait: a companion who hears or observes something intended for him and ignores it is said to be "no fly".

"No, You Don't!"-This means that information given, or relation of' action taken, is not believed by the others present; and heads are shaken as the words go forth: "No, You Don't!"

On the Coach.-In stage-coach travelling times, if one person wished to avoid another during the journey he would seek an inside seat while the other had perforce to travel outside high up on the coach. If two compositors fall out (publicly or privately) they avoid each other. Companions are quick to notice this in Chapel, and the word goes round:' "Bill's got Jasper on the coach".

On the Stone.-Taking a compositor away from one class of work and putting him at work on a page waiting to be sent to press. The stone is an imposing surface on which pages are prepared for press. It is of metal but was formerly a flat stone.

Pica-Thumpers.-For the benefit of laymen, "Pica" refers to a size of type used in the old days largely for Parliamentary and similar work. Thumping was the lifting of the types from the cases into the composing sticks. Hence, "pica-thumpers", a term applying, in fact, to all hand piece-workers. The coming of the composing machine displaced them.

Piece Work.-Work paid for at the rates laid down in the piece scales.

Pieing Your Case.-To pie a case is accidentally to mix the letters so that they have to be sorted out and put in the right boxes.

Putting the Line On.-When compositors are engaged on piece work each must be ready to start to set his first line when the Father calls "Line On". Copy is lifted simultaneously and work begins. This is known as the "simultaneous lift" and is strictly observed in daily paper companionships.

Putting up the Half-Double.-A half-double rule was always printed at the end of an article; nowadays half-singles are the fashion. Therefore "to put up the half-double" is to end conversation on a particular subject between compositors.

Ratting.-Is working under the recognised price.

Spiking.-When copy is left incomplete, or taken away before the article is finished, it is "spiked"; and if it is returned later the compositor to whom it is given to resume setting calls it "taking up the spike".

'Stab Work.-Work paid for at the established weekly rate.

Takes.-A "take" is a piece of copy set by the compositor.

The House.-This means the Society house; the offices of the London Society of Compositors.

The Organ.-A mutual club formed by compositors and paid for by them at so much per week, enabling those who wish, to borrow money and repay with interest to the secretary, or Organ Master, as he is known.

The Printer, or the "O".-A Printer of a paper-that is; he who is in charge and is responsible for seeing the pages off the stone to the foundry or the machine-is known as "the Bloke". So is an overseer of a composing room. He who is responsible for the paper is called a Printer, while the overseer may be responsible for a great variety of jobs, but is never called the Printer.

"The Slate is Up".-A slate is provided in each office where piece workers are employed. When a compositor finishes his "take" and finds no more COPY to lift, he writes his name on the slate and waits for work, calling out, "Slate Up". When there is more copy, "takes" are lifted in the order of names on the slate.

The Swinger.-The last "take" of copy in the box is termed "the swinger", and to "grab the swinger" is to drop the "take" just set and get to the copy box before other striving companions, who have disconsolately to put up the slate.

Trotting.-Leading a companion "up the garden path".

Wayzgoose.-An Outing, Before WW2 this usually took place to a seaside resort like Margate or Blackpool. Can also apply to an evening out together for say, a slap-up meal.

Whack!-When compositors are gathered together and a tall story is told, or it be doubted that the truth has been told by a speaker, a whack with the composing stick on the frame is given as an indication of unphilosophic doubt.

Wrong Cast-Off.-To estimate something incorrectly. A compositor will say to another who has made a wrong statement through guesswork; "You've made a wrong cast-off".

You Can!-This is a phrase that increases or decreases in effect by inflection as it is pronounced. It means that the speaker presents to his hearers the whole matter under discussion for them to do with as they wish. There was once a compositor who was called "You Can Have It Jones" on account of his deprecatory attitude to the whole universe.

Hot Metal in Australia

By Arthur Johnson

I STARTED my apprenticeship in 1953 at Winn & Co in Sydney Australia a medium sized shop with 2 Linotypes a Model 8 electric pot and a 4! with a gas pot. There was also an old 21m Ludlow and a Model K Elrod which I worked and serviced.

I worked mainly as a stone hand doing imposition for the big Miehles and Heidelbergs.

I learnt a little about operating and later did a course at the Ultimo School of Graphic Arts on the Lino.

I worked at several places as a Comp Operator and had my own business with a Model 15 single magazine machine.

I left the trade in 1975 and later trained as an Enrolled Nurse. When I semi retired 4 years ago the local museum at Gulgong NSW had a small print display with no one to work it.

I offered to do it and now we have a great display of Hot Metal Machines and Letterpress Printing.

We have a C3 Intertype, Model 48 Linotype, Ludlow and a Elrod, all except the Elrod are Running and in regular use.

My experience with the linecasters is limited and sometimes it's hard for me to sort things out, the internet with other interested people are a great help.

I will be starting our local show programme on the C3 and 48 this week 92 pages and cover (at least some is standing from last year) great fun and I really enjoy working with the machines of my youth.

I hope to teach others to work the machines, at least the Ludlow, I can see it being used long after the C3 and 48.

Fleet Street Piecework

by Malcolm Gregory

I WAS working on an Intertype at the Walthamstow Guardian when I managed to get a 'Grass' on the Sunday Telegraph (this meant working the Saturday as a casual operator) through a fellow operator who put in a word, knowhatimean?

It was a real closed society when I started, no-one told new people anything and bearing in mind that it was piecework and a docket had to be filled out for every slug of type set and there were three separate type of charges this meant you were really in the dark.

Eventually one of the older regular operators took pity on me and showed me how to charge my work, anyway that is what I thought until I found he was copying what I was charging and also charging it himself!

Anyway, I persevered not knowing if I would be called back the next Saturday until last knockings Saturday night. Hardly any of the regulars spoke to us lower forms of life but I needed the money so I kept my head down until out of the blue I was asked if I was interested in a 'spike' on the Daily Telegraph night shift (called the Continuity).

As this trebled my wages from the Walthamstow Guardian I didn't say no. When I told my wife she said that I shouldn't take that amount of money each week as it was too much!

When I started I wasn't allowed to write a piece docket until they felt I was fast enough (and could earn enough) for their pooled piece work. Then they had a Chapel meeting (without me) and decided if they wanted me in. Fortunately they voted me in and I was there for the next 15 years.

When I started I made the mistake of putting up my own ingot and got jumped on by the local Natsopa bloke whose sole job it was to do that. I also learned that the liners mustn't be changed by the operators, although we were allowed to fix the disser stops and splashes. Most of the machines were Linotype 48s with later Intertypes with Mohr saws for the ads in the 'Monkey House' (a small room attached to the Linotype room).

The Chapel ruled the whole area and the Printers kept their heads down, this encouraged the characters of the department (mostly compositors as we were too busy writing our dockets earning money). There were untold 'trots' (I think wind-up would be a contemporary analogy) A good one was a reel of toy gun 'caps' strapped round the main drive cog so when a line is sent away a machine gun like effect took place, this almost stopped the operator writing a charge, but in the end we developed a charge specially for this event!

The Father of the Chapel was the King of the whole place and to be truthful he didn't do a lot of work, but he did the negotiating so he was given that privilege. He approved hiring and firing and untold numbers of Chapel Meetings.

I can honestly say that I enjoyed every night I went to work and looking back how privileged we were to be in that position for such a long time. Eventually it all went t*ts up, but these things happen, it certainly gave me a good living for a long period of time and was the best place I have ever 'worked.'

Sunday Telegraph Grass Ship
by George Clark

MALCOLM GREGORY paints a very black picture of the S.T. Grass Ship, as one who served on this Ship from April 1964 retiring as a "Regular" on 29th March 1986 I feel I should give a clearer picture.

To go back somewhat earlier. I was invited to Oversee the installation of the first two 42-em Intertype C4s and take charge of the resulting Ship at Burrup Mathieson (now known as "Burrups"), in 1958. The Ship grew at a phenomenal rate to become eight Intertype machines with 16 Operators under my charge eight on Days and eight on Nights.

My qualifications for this amounted to a two-year Evening Course at the London School of Printing as Operator/Mechanic and having "done the rounds" of various single installations in the General Trade. Around the early 1960s I was learning from some of my operators about a List of Grasshands which was compiled by the NGA (I had been a member since the days of the London Society of Compositors). I thought I would try it out and applied to "The House" to be placed on the List.

An explanation of Grass Ships may be useful here. There existed in those days a number of "Solo Sundays", i.e. Newspapers located in Fleet Street and surrounding areas which were not tied to a "Daily", to the best of my knowledge now, they were the Sunday Telegraph, Sunday Times, People, Observer and News of the World. Most had small Grass Ships ranging from four to six or eight Operators, the Sunday Telegraph was the largest with 20 Operators.

I count myself as fortunate in that I was selected for the S.T. Malcolm Gregory is correct in stating that one started in a casual capacity, covering for Operators sick or on holiday. As members left the regular 20 for various reasons the senior "casual" was promoted to the regular 20, my opportunity arose after about six months. On my first day I met up with an old colleague, Les Mervish, who had been an Operator at Burrups but moved on. I do not think this helped me particularly but I found both the fellow Grasshands and Regulars a very friendly bunch who never hesitated to educate me on the intricacies of the S.T.'s particular brand of charging. Also I would point out that there was always the Tracker who would analyse our Dockets during the passing week and "beard" us the following Saturday over any overcharging which he suspected.

Around lunchtime, Les came around to me and asked how I was getting on. I remarked, "Fine, I am enjoying myself very well." His reply was "it'll 'get you' you know." How right he was, there is a certain atmosphere on a "National" which does not exist in the General Trade. So far as the "Society" was concerned, Fleet Street Newspapers came under a separate heading known as the News Department, this did not apply to Weekly Newspapers who were part of the General Trade.

At the time of my completing my Apprenticeship around 1949 Apprentices were encouraged to leave and move on around the General Trade. No two Printing Offices functioned exactly the same and some specialised in a particular class of work. Moving around undoubtedly improved one's knowledge and broadened one's experience. It was as a result of this that I learnt a lot about Piecework although I never actually experienced it. I certainly never had problems with Charging when I joined the S.T. and there were always both Grasshands and Regulars ready to "take me under their wing".

On the point of charging Piece in relation to the Grass Ship there were a number of "fat takes", by this I mean, with those particular "takes", tabular work for which one made extra charges, for changes of fount or mould size which although done for you by the Engineer carried charges for the time taken, etc.

Fat Takes

One received such "fat takes" in order of seniority, moving from one to another as your seniority changed. This generally meant moving to a different regular machine which was dedicated to a particular task. A few machines carried a 9pt. fount and mould. If you were moved to one of these machines you got the 9×1 intros with extra charges for Drop Initials, Byline, and in my earlier days the Dateline, plus the normal "take and change". One lucky Operator eventually got on the machine carrying 12×2, this would cover double-column intros, if you got a 12×2 into 12×1 this would give one an extra charge for turning in the Vice Jaws to single column, the Random Hand cut the slugs down to single column on a Slug Saw.

In particular, I remember not only the aforementioned Les Mervish but Ernie Haswell, at that time both had a Mon.-Fri. job at the Stratford Express. Later Ernie moved on I believe to a National Daily which ruled him out from grassing. Les moved on to a Mon.-Fri. job at the Radio Times which meant that he could still continue grassing.

Over the years I made many friends of most of the Grasshands and Regulars alike whom I still consider as good friends today although I have lost touch with most. I recall, on the last day of Hot Metal, when we knew most of the machines were going for scrap I took the liberty of removing the plate off the distributor-beam on one of the Model 78s, it is still a treasured possession. Soon after the cessation of Hot Metal, arrangements were made for an annual Reunion, these were held at the "Cartoonist" in Shoe Lane on the first week in December each year.

Whilst I continued to live in South Lambeth I attended every one, it was sad to see faces disappear each year as the older members passed away but we all enjoyed meeting up again. I moved North in September 1995 to South West Scotland. Unfortunately the first week in December has turned out to be busy for me locally so I am unable to attend the Reunions if they still continue.

Malcolm Gregory seems to give an equally dark picture of the Chapel situation at the S.T., I would also dispute this. We had a Grasshands Chapel, my first FOC was Tony Crichton Smith, his name may have been more familiar to Comps. and Operators as A. R. Smith, whose name cropped up on a lot of Society matter around the early 1960s. The Lino FOC was Eric Gregory, another old friend now sadly deceased. He was later elected to the post of Imperial FOC and Derek Chapman succeeded him as Lino FOC, all very approachable people.

Malcolm Gregory also bewails the fact that he was "pulled up" for hanging up his Ingots, changing up Moulds, etc. I respectfully suggest that if he had moved around the General Trade a bit more he would have been fully aware of these things. That happened on all large Installations where they had Lino Assistants (his Natsopas), and Linotype Engineers.

In my comparatively small Installation at Burrups the Operators did quite a number of jobs forbidden in the larger Installations. Namely cleaning Pots, Plungers and Spacebands before starting a shift. For these tasks they were generally allowed one hour on their Dockets. Even at the Kentish Times where I did nine months off the Casual List after redundancy, we did our own work on our machines and that was an Installation of 20 machines with no Lino Assistants or Engineers, just an Operator/Mechanic in charge.

Of life on the Daily Telegraph I can say little. In the days of Hot Metal the two papers were completely separate entities although I believe they were merged upon the move to West Ferry Road and Canada Wharf. One particularly good friend that I left behind at Peterborough Court was Doug Allen, Engineer. We first met when he came from Intertype, Slough, to install the first Intertype C4 which I had installed for me after numerous frustrating years with a 6SM Linotype at the firm where I served my Apprenticeship, where I returned as an Operator for about seven years.

From then on I think every Intertype wherever I worked was installed by Doug. It included the initial two machines at Burrups. They were two of the first three 42-em machines built after WW2 and they caused a lot of teething troubles due to the fact that all the engineers who had worked on the pre-war 42-em machines were no longer working at Intertype. Doug and I worked hard to iron out the faults and we must have succeeded since the later 42-em machines (the Grey machines), were an absolute pleasure to work.

As the "New Tech" revolution gained pace Intertype passed dealings with their Hot Metal machines to Linotype & Machinery to concentrate on New Tech. As a result Doug, in company with the other Engineers became redundant. Imagine my surprise when he arrived at the Sunday Telegraph to work as an Engineer there. He was a great asset since I think it is fair to say that the Linotype-trained Engineers never really came to terms with the subtle differences of the Intertypes. The Intertypes never worked so well as they did after Doug's arrival.

I have not said a lot on how we did things at Peterborough Court but I feel I should not hog too much space. Perhaps I will return to tell some of the more intimate side of the Sunday Telegraph Linotypes and Intertypes at a later date.

Advance Memories

by Albert W Perez

In MARCH, 1973, I started my apprenticeship with The Daily Advance in Dover, New Jersey. My father, 3 uncles and 2 aunts had worked in the trade, so for me, it was a natural.

The Daily Advance was a 5 day-a-week morning paper with a circulation of around 25,000. Four Linotypes, 2 Ludlows, a 3 unit letterpress, the oldest unit dating to 1908.

Most of the Lino operators and compositors working there were older, many having worked at the big New York City newspapers at one time or another.

Many were hard drinking, colourful characters. But one stood out from all the others, Louis Nazarro.

Louis had started working for the Advance as a 21 year old apprentice. He retired from the Advance at age 71, the prototypical dirty old man.

Louis was about 5 feet 2 inches tall. Every day he came to work dressed in an overcoat, hat, jacket and tie. His shoes were always shined.

He would go to his locker, change his clothes, put on his apron and proceed to greet his fellow workers.

Morning, Governor, What's New?

He greeted everyone with a different expression, but always the same one every day. Mine was "Morning Governor, what's new?"

For over 5 years until he retired it was the same. I developed a response. "Not much, and you?"

So on it went, day after day, even when I worked the night shift and would see him in the locker room as he was coming and I was going. "Morning Governor, what's new." "Not much, and you?"

Louis was the prototypical lecher. He thought nothing of dropping his line gauge on the floor if it might afford a look up a girl's skirt.

He was big on cheap thrills.

He loved to tell stories of his days as a youth, when he and his friends would take the train from Dover to Scranton, PA, to spend the weekend running the red light district.

Even into his sixties he would make a monthly trip to New York City to procure a certain service his wife wouldn't provide.

Louis was one of the many colourful people I met working there.

The drunk West Indian editor who loved to spend time in the composing room, spouting philosophy and engaging in sharp political debate.

The divorced, female, senior editor who loved to hire, and seduce, young male reporters.

The deaf typesetter who became my friend and taught me sign language.

Louis is gone, the Daily Advance is gone, typography is gone, my youth is gone.

But I'll always have these wonderful memories.

New Zealand Novice

by Graeme How

IT WAS late 1969. After a year of getting used to the layout of the Californian hand set type cases, I was sat down in front of one of our linotypes.

My big moment had arrived; I was actually going to operate one of the 'eight wonders of the world.' My only association with the linotypes up to this moment was cleaning the spacebands, plungers and plunger wells. "Follow the copy, even if it flies out the window", Jack said, (who had been operating linotypes since before the Second World War).

My hands were shaking as they hovered over the keyboard, and for the first time I noticed that there were no letters showing on that keyboard. They had worn away after decades of use. "How am I supposed to learn the keyboard with no letters on it?" I asked. "The bloody hard way," came the reply.

So after copying the keyboard layout from one of the Intertypes onto a piece of cardboard I began to set straight news copy using 8 point (can't remember the typeface) on a ten em measure. I was in hot metal heaven.

The months past, I was then 'promoted' to the Intertype with the side magazine and keyboard and let loose on classified and display advertising, followed by jobbing work for our commercial print department.

This machine was the ultimate, it had a quadder. Type sizes ranged from 6 to 36 point. The 36 point type had to be hand assembled in a special setting stick and placed in the elevator jaw to be cast into a slug.

The day came when I could 'hang' the machine (assemble a line, have the machine casting, and matrices being distributed, all at once) on a 20 em measure setting 8 point type. Only then, I thought that I was a pretty good operator.

Being an operator in a small rural town meant you also had to be the mechanic. This made the job more interesting and varied.

Having progressed through the photosetting and paste up technologies and now operating computers using PageMaker and PhotoShop, I look back on the hot metal days as some of the happiest in my working career.

Who else but hot metal operators could go home with burn scars on their hands after a 'splash' and the girlfriend of the time complaining because you threw your lead splattered jeans into the washing machine.

Short Memories

We had a compositor who could never get the Lino to cast a line. Every time he sat down at the keyboard, one of us operators would sneak around behind the machine and pull the plunger pin out.

Winter time in New Zealand can be cold at times. To keep our pies or burgers warm we used to sit them on top of the melting pot and they would travel backwards and forwards on the pot as the slugs were being cast.

School children would tour our newspaper and marvel at the linotypes. Even today, as adults they come up to me and say they remember the linotypes and the smell of lead and ink.

Three times a year we had to work nights to set the racing form guide for the local jockey club. The pages were printed on a 'Kelly' press in eight page impositions. The printer had to check the proofs before the pages were printed. After checking the first press run proofs, he would go and have a coffee break. While he was having his coffee break one of us would unlock the chase and turn one of the pages upside down. After his break, he would start the press, and after a couple of hundred impressions or so the bad language would start, after he discovered one of the pages was upside down. He tried to blame us, but we just laughed and told him to check his work before starting the press. This happened year after year, and he could not understand why this was happening. We told him why when he retired. After calling us a pack of bastards, he could see the funny side.

One of our editors could sit at the lino and 'direct input' his copy. The unions used to frown on that practice, but what they didn't know, couldn't hurt.

The Linotype Mechanic
by Keith Prentice

IN 1948 I was indentured as a Linotype mechanic apprentice at The Otago Daily Times in Dunedin, New Zealand and trained on Model 8 & 14 Linotypes as well as Intertype C3 , C4, and G4-4sm machines. I also operated an Elrod strip caster.

I went to Australia in 1954 and joined the mechanic staff at the Herald-Sun in Melbourne and maintained Linotype Model 8 and 48 machines and Intertype C4s. I spent a short period working with The Courier-Mail in Brisbane with a battery of similar machines.

Returning to New Zealand in 1957 I spent two years with a firm of Typesetters maintaining Linotype Model 32s, an Intertype Model F mixer and a C4 with a six mold disc.

In 1959 I joined Gollin Graphics, the NZ agency for Harris-Intertype. During a period of 23 years as Installation & Service Engineer I installed every model of Intertype including Monarch throughout the country. Pacific Island installations included, Fiji, Tonga and Tahiti.

I received Monarch machine training at Harris-Intertype in Furman St, Brooklyn, New York and installed 12 of these machines in NZ, some of which were operated with Star Autosetter and Star Quadder.

42 em Intertypes

Over the years I rebuilt a number of Intertypes including Model A & B machines. We even had a few 42 em Intertypes in the country but I preferred to steer clear of them. My work in the field included installing Mohr Saw units, Star Quadders and Autosetters.

My last Intertype installation took place in Tahiti in 1974 but I was kept employed by the company, importing spare parts and matrices until 1982. The change in technology at this point made it necessary for me to seek new challenges outside of the industry.

I have enjoyed the experience and have been fortunate being able to work in many locations and work along side a huge variety of people, many of them unforgettable characters.

It Was One of Those Days
by David Andrus

It was one of those days
the machine began to act up,
th troubl somwhr in
th distributor mchanism,
nd I only begn to notice it
when my proofs cme bck
nd the proofreder's red ink
ran frm my type like blod
frm a slaughtered pg,
lke paint frm Van Ggh's
Hed of A Womn,
and the sharp, terrile lines
wounded me at my machin,
so that siting a the keord
I flt like a World War II fighter plot
going down with hi craft,
in front f me th burning lead
scummd ovr with dust nd
dross, al of it trembling
bcuse of a slightly-loos
driv blt, and th day
ending badly when the elevatr
jammed and a spurt f lead
ejaculated int the air and
came down on my head lik
hot hot rain,
nd now as I get oldr
and baldr, the smll burn scars
becme mor and mor visible,
remindng me of tht day
th machine began to act up

and finlly hurt me
hurt m bdly

The Machine

by David Andrus

1954:
Central S.S., Hamilton
The Linotype is just a machine
we are told
like any other machine.
But this is wrong-
at the age of 14 I am
captivated by this ungainly
word-making device,
seduced by its handles,
wheels, pulleys, gears, cams,
fingers, arms and jaws,
its thousand mysteries of
brass and steel.
And for a decade
we grapple at a distance,
the machine and I,
its secrets whispered to me
by men with wooden legs,
men born in other centuries.
It is the first obsession
to shake me,
and carries me into time
locked against its molten heart,
troubling my dreams
again and again,
and again near the end,
as the machine stumbles on
its iron feet,
plunges from its pinnacle
into the soft, deep pages next to
Gutenberg and his moveable type.

1982:
Seldon Printing, Hamilton
the last machine is hauled into
the street and sold for scrap metal.

E for Exasperation!

by Dean Nayes

DURING my travels across the United States I came across a very ingenious Linotype operator.

He had taken a lower case e matrix, cut it out, turned it upside down, and somehow managed to restore the mat so it would cast within a line all right.

At times, when a new operator was working, he would insert this lower case e into the magazine of his machine, leave it for some time, then retrieve it without the operator knowing.

Soon, the galley proofs would come back to the new operator, with a lower case e upside down.

He would be instructed to run out all the lower case e's and cast a line so they could find the culprit.

But, of course, there was no upside down e, leaving the operator wondering what in the hell happened to his machine.

The Green Card

by Dean Nayes

BACK in 1968, after 13 years of "homesteading", I decided I was going on the road again.

I went to Sacramento, slipped up on the Bee, and was working nights operating. I was about ready to return to the midwest, and one of my old traveling buddies came to me and said, "Dean, there is a kid in the ad room, who just finished his apprenticeship in one of the small papers somewhere up the Truckee River, and he wants to go on the road, to get some more experience, and I was wondering if you would mind taking him with you."

He introduced him to me, we talked for a while and decided to take off together in my pickup. We started toward Reno, on the way to Salt Lake again, but were stopped about half way up the mountain because of a blizzard, and we could not find chains for the truck. We turned around and headed for L.A., going the southern route.

We slipped up at the LA Examiner. They had posted on the chapel slipboard, that negotiations had ceased, and it looked like they would be going on strike very soon. We didn't quite have as much money as we needed to travel east, so we slipped up at the Green Sheet in Burbank.

We worked a couple of weeks, and were ready to go, so I called the chairman over to where I was inserting classified ads into the iron chases, liners, prior to making up the pages. I asked the chairman if we could cash out in the morning, pick up our check and travelers, and be on our way.

Company policy

He informed me that it was company policy that the only time we could get our checks was pay day, they would not cash us out. I asked him to get the foreman, and he complied. I repeated my request to the foreman, and he gave me the same answer, and added, that we could leave an address, and the company would send our checks to us. I informed him that we didn't know where we were going, therefore, I could give him no address.

Then I had an idea, so I informed the foreman that if he fired me, by state law, the company would have to pay me in full, within 24 hours. He replied, that he had no intention of firing me. So I grabbed the side screw on the chase I was working on, and it was on a turtle, I put my foot on the turtle and shoved a bit while holding the chase screw.

The chase was about half full of classified liners. I glanced up at the foreman and said, "If I go ahead and push this turtle out from under this chase, you will fire me, and the company will pay me tomorrow." He began begging me not to spill that page of liners all over the composing room floor. I said, "not until I am assured that we can pick up our checks tomorrow."

Well, we left the next afternoon with our checks, and I don't think that it hurt that company at all, taking a few minutes to figure two employees earnings a few days early.

Pennsylvania Pre-Press
by Thomas A Berkheiser

MY NAME is Thomas A. Berkheiser, from Paxinos, Pennsylvania.

My father was a linotype operator for fifty years, and worked at the Shamokin News-Dispatch, in Shamokin, Pennsylvania, where I started in 1964 as an apprentice with the International Typographical Union.

I learned to operate the Linotype at the newspaper, and also went into photocomp, but I'd rather operate a Linotype any day!!!

We only had one Intertype, it was an Intertype Mixer, purchased by the newspaper around 1968, I never had the chance to operate it, although I would have loved to have had a chance.

We had what we called five automatics, run by perforated tape, and 12 other Linotypes in the newspaper that I worked at in 1970, where I was laid off because of the new phototypesetting equipment that was brought into the newspaper.

I'm 57 years old, and wish I could get back into printing, when it gets into your blood, it never goes away.

Books in Bloomsburg

I also worked at a book publishing plant in Bloomsburg, Pa. with many type fonts to choose from. We had many, many, magazines, with old style figures, new style figures, etc.

I did a lot of caps and small cap work, only a Linotype operator would understand this. I also set a book in German, not understanding the language, although I am of German descent.

I would like to get a Linotype or Intertype just to set in my basement. I also used a Ludlow many a time. I'm proud to be of the few left that understands these machines, like up on the rail typesetting.

I was proficient in both computer typesetting and Linotype typesetting, and I established a training class for the older men, because I heard they wanted to keep the younger men, and let the older guys go, one of which was my father!

I helped train the men, and I left with a clean conscience.

We have some Linotypes still operating in some small Job Shops in the area.

It's nice to see there are still some people out there that have the same interests that I have! Thank you for giving me a chance to get involved with this project.

Salt Lake Deadline

by Dean Nayes

IN 1956, myself, and a friend, Joe McGowan, left the Rocky Mountain News in February, after the Xmas layoffs.

We first hit Casper Wyoming, worked a few days, to get some money in the kick, then to Cheyenne for a few more shifts.

We then landed in Salt Lake City, slipped up on the Tribune as operators.

Now, I have to tell you that Joe was getting up in age, and wasn't one of the swiftest operators. Before we went to work, the foreman called us into his office and gave us each a style book.

He informed us what the deadline, (amount of lines needed per shift to be deemed a competent operator) was.

Can we go home?

I asked him, "can we go home when we reach the deadline?" He answered, "no." I stated, "why are you telling me what it is, if I cannot go home when I reach it?" We went to work and finished the shift. The next afternoon, when we showed for work, the foreman came over and handed each of us a slip of paper with a figure written on it.

I looked at it and asked, "what is this?" He replied, "That is the lineage each of you set last night."

Mine was within about 50 lines off the deadline, but Joe's was quite a bit less than that.

The foreman stated that he could live with my output, that he knew I could make the deadline, but that he didn't think Joe could make it.

I told him that we were just going to work that night, and leave for San Francisco the next day, so he hired

Joe as an operator, and I worked the ad room that night. That was 1956.

In February, 1975, my wife and I slipped up there again, the foreman came over, looked at me, and said, "I know you, you are the guy who wanted to go home when you reached the deadline." We had a huge laugh about that.

A Measured Approach

by Dean Nayes

I RETURNED to the Salt Lake Tribune just a few months after going through the first time, on my way back to Denver, to get my family, and return to San Francisco.

I worked a few shifts in both directions. It was at the time that the Tribune had either just purchased the Deseret News, or they had merged, I don't remember which.

They had moved all of the production of the News to the Tribune, along with dovetailing the priority board in the composing room.

There was some bickering about the dovetailing, and other pressures in that shop that I don't quite remember, but when I sat down at my machine, I noticed the operator next to me take his line gauge and measure each take before he dumped it, and he wrote it down on a pad.

He did this all night, until shortly before quitting time, when I saw him measure his take again, he took half of the type he had set and threw it in the hell box, and dumped the rest.

When he returned, I asked him what he was doing. He answered, "They dupe us every night, everybody, and I keep track of my lineage, and when I reach the deadline, I refuse to set any more, and if I set too much I will dump it in the hell box."

There were a lot of Mormons who came from the News, and I believe this fellow was one of them because they all wore overalls.

The deadline there was one of the toughest I had ever encountered, because the Deseret News, being a

Mormon newspaper, had more obits in it than any other paper I had ever worked on, and just about every one had a thumbnail picture in it that you had to wrap the type around, in agate, classified measure.

There were a lot of good operators who could not make the deadline there. But it was a very good place to stop and pick up a couple of shifts when you were traveling, because you could hit town by show up time, work a shift, and the chairman would cash you out at the end of the shift, and issue you a new traveler, and you could be back on the road again.

Dying Days
by Alan Young

STARTED my career at Wolf Composition in Reading, Massachusetts, USA in 1964.

First I pulled proofs in this book shop. Then I graduated to the linotype.

Finished up my apprenticeship (ITU) in 1971, just in time to get laid off due to the company moving the bulk of its production to England.

From there I went to the ITU's Training Center in Colorado Springs, CO. Never used the training I got there as I learned there was plenty of work in Denver.

So went back to Massachusetts to get a traveler and my stuff and out to Denver. Slipped up at The Denver Post summer of 1972. Made the mistake of leaving a few months later and ended up at the Cape Cod Standard Times in Hyannis.

When spring came decided to try my luck out in Portland, Oregon. Not much there so I went back to Denver and the Post. Things were fine until new technology reared its head.

After a few stints with what linotype typesetting was left (mostly fly-by-night), landed a full time steady job at the Leadville (Colorado) Herald Democrat running a Model 5.

This went fine until the publisher decided to retire and sold to a regional chain. New technology again with no place for me.

This was the summer of 1985. And this is when I knew it was over. I still at times long for the days I ran a linotype.

This is basically my story as one of the last linotype operators.

Bridlington Chronicle

by Mike Wilson

MY EAGLE CLUB DIARY has the following note for Monday, 8th September, 1952: "Started work at 8. Did metal for Linotype. 12-1 dinner. Left at 4.30." On Thursday the 11th: "After dinner went to sorting office." I remember why that was noted. The papers sent by post were rolled up, wrapped and addressed in the office, but I had to trundle them to the sorting office. On a station-type wheelbarrow with iron wheels. What a racket! I was sure my mother could hear me back at home on the other side of town! When a postman saw me stuffing them into the postbox near the post office door, he showed me round the back to the sorting office.

But then, I was a grammar school lad, with a smattering of German, Latin, algebra, biology and English Literature. I soon found out how little I knew of the ways of the world when I was asked to "mek us some tea, lad." There was a disgusting sink in one corner where the machine men washed their rollers with paraffin which had a cold tap. I held the kettle under there as though I would be poisoned. And the teapot! And the mugs! Good grief! My mother would have thrown a wobbly if she'd seen them. Anyway we all survived. But it's taken me until nearly retirement to have a cup of my tea drunk without comment.

I remember on one occasion I was keying away merrily, when my tutor, Neil Jemison, watched me. He had a small oilcan in his hand which he used to flush out muck from various places on the Intertype. As he passed the front of my machine, he squirted the contents of the can on to the gas flames at the throat of the metal pot. Whoosh! Up went a sheet of flame, and back went my chair, throwing me on to the floor.

Another trick for the concentrating and unwary operator: Just as the ejector is about to push out the slug, the way is clear for the perpetrator to whack the top of the level sharply. The ejector moves forward much more quickly than usual and the slug comes onto the delivery slide like a rocket, with an accompanying clatter.

One operator I knew had an evening job in a bar, leaving him short of sleep. During the afternoon when his eyelids were heavy, he would rest the base of his hands onto the bottom of the keyboard, keeping his fingers off the keys. He'd pretend to be studying the copy. He'd do this once or twice then carry on working. But occasionally he'd try it once too often. His eyelids would close, and he'd nod off. After a second, his fingers would lower, contact the keys and in a second all manner of matrices would clatter into the assembler, waking him up with a start! It became so frequent that we other operators would pass the word along the line and we'd watch him. Somehow nobody seemed to care.

One Thursday a local newsagent rang up and asked for extra copies of the paper. This was unheard of. Anyway, I was sent round with another dozen and he greeted me with a smile. "Have you seen it, lad?" I didn't know what he was talking about. So he showed me the advert inside. And there it was: "Boys' Summer Shirts." But without the "r" in the last word!

I was deferred from National Service until my five years' apprenticeship was complete. For a short while I attended evening classes for Linotype Mechanics. This meant an evening train ride to Hull, where I visited the Hull Daily Mail building to get my hands on screwdrivers and such. I was awarded a micrometer at the end of my "course," and it still lurks in my "slum." (I picked up this word when at Aylesbury. All the London overspill men used the term for that special place everyone has where all the bits and pieces, odds and sods, "things that'll come in handy," are kept). I have three slums in my cabinet alongside my PC.

Mechanics did not come easy. I am not naturally gifted with machines and how they work. I can work them well. I can drive but am useless when I lift the bonnet. I was the same on the Linos. I could keep them punching out line after line with no difficulty, but when they stopped I struggled. I reckoned I learned sufficiently of the day-to-day maintenance and upkeep of the Linotype and was eventually skilled enough to take out a quadder, clean it and replace it correctly. The major pieces of the machine though, they were beyond me.

Not only did I "do" the metal for the Linotype on my first day, but probably every Monday for the next two years. One day the metal pot downstairs had been filled with last week's metal, the gas burner lit, and left to do its job. After a while I came downstairs only to find that the tap hadn't been closed properly the last time it was used, and molten lead had run across the floor like water, finding indentations in the concrete.

All those operators who have bent liners because they forgot to change the ejector blade have my sympathy. I bent one once and incurred the huge wrath of the foreman. I was left in no doubt what type of idiot I was. We managed to replace the liner, and I sent the next line away. Whoops! Who'd forgotten to change the ejector blade? Was it me or him? Another liner gone.

I dread to think how much running those Linotypes cost. Bent matrices, battered spacebands. The number of hours spent on the step at the back clearing the disser, cleaning up after a splash, faffing about with ingots of metal, and cleaning spacebands. Of all the jobs to do, well that was the worst. Loose graphite all over, three or four operators all using the same piece of plywood covered in that fine black powder. It got up your nose, up your sleeves, all over the front of your overall. And the management had to allow half an hour for the job. So it was used as a good skive. Then, of course, there was "cleaning the plunger," another daily routine. And "scraping the well." I can't believe how much I remember!

And what about washing mats? Matrices, of course. We used an old enamel bowl which had definitely seen better days, half full of petrol. We put the mats in and swilled them round. Picked a matrix up and rubbed it between the fingers until the muck came away. Repeat. Ad infinitum it seemed. I don't think anyone smoked when that job was being done, but it wouldn't surprise me if they did. Nowadays I reckon Health & Safety would have had that stopped.

I have copies of the last issue of the Bridlington Chronicle and two sets of copper blocks used for printing the masthead. When we stopped producing the newspaper, we chucked everyone out of the windows into a yard below, where it was taken away for scrap. When I took this photo my back is against a Columbian press, the one with an eagle on top.

And here's a question for all visitors to the site. Could a Linotype be built from scratch today? The books I have show an extremely complex machine, with a huge lump of unsophisticated cast iron supporting the most elegantly engineered steel components. I honestly don't think any top-rate engineer, even with unlimited time, equipment and funds at his disposal, would be able to build one. I know there are examples still working out there, but to build one from scratch? I don't think it can be done. If it actually could, at what price?

Letterpress Limericks

by Greg Fischer

A machinist who came from Timor
Changed magazines often before.
But the lock wasn't tight
To the left, but was right.
And he dumped mats all over the floor.

--::--

A Linotype man from L.A.
Was having a difficult day.
With fingers abused
ETAOIN was used
And SHRDLU brought into play.

--::--

A newspaper man from LaCrosse
Saw his paper ran at a loss.
He hollered "Oh No!
My Hoe is too slow!
" And traded it in for a Goss.

--::--

An Intertype gal from LeMans
Sets type with both of her hands.
And sometimes her toes
And the tip of her nose.
Whatever production demands.

--::--

A nasty old pressman I knew
Got to hell without much ado.
Satan said "You have sinned,"
As he devilishly grinned "
What a press I've here waiting for you!"

--::--

A German man quite laconic

Would print things only teutonic.
Like instructions for strudels
Sauerbraten with noodles
And notes for the Bonn Philharmonic.
--::--
A short-legged man from Seville
Built his shop on the side of a hill.
After printing away
For a year and a day
He discovered one leg shorter still.
--::--
A printer who lives in Sudan
Runs his press just as fast as he can.
To make matters worse
He once ran in reverse
And finished before he began.
--::--
A pressman who's now in perdition
Came to work in a drunken condition.
He fell in the press
Which made quite a mess.
It was surely his final edition.
--::--
A fellow who worked in Pocasset
Printed a job for the Knesset.
It didn't delight
For it read left to right
Which was backwards, but he didn't guess it.
--::--
"My press" said a printer in Ghent
"Was pedaled so fast that it bent.
This meddlesome treadle
Unsettled my mettle,
So for one from John Hern I have sent."
--::--
At the Linotype he was quite new.
Did not know quite what to do.

A careless tight line
Brought a scream, then a whine
As typemetal spattered his shoe.
--::--
There once was a man from Luzerne
Who did printing carelessly learn.
With a slip of the wrist
By his press he was kissed
And he no longer can "Work and turn."
--::--
A printer who worked in Lahore
Had legs all tired and sore.
"If I had but a Kimble
I could be quite nimble
For I would treadle no more."
--::--
A printer in Hades from Islet
Soon by the devil was met.
Who with eyes all agleam
Said "Take this machine,
You've an acre of agate to set."
--::--
An engraver, an unhappy wretch
Had a problem he just couldn't catch.
He said "I don't know
Why this bath works so slow,
But this looks like a seven year etch."
--::--
"Be a six year apprentice" they said.
"With a permanent job just ahead.
" But his joy soon diminished
As soon as he finished.
"Going cold type, hot metal is dead!"
--::--
A printer who worked in Bangkok
Had a turtle he kept in his shop.
Not the kind you might know

That walks pretty slow
But with wheels and cast iron top.
--::--

An Intertype man from Alsace
When involved in a typesetting race,
Yelled "I'll win in a breeze!"
As smoke rose from the keys
And he set a blistering pace.
He set type in total confusion.
His skills were just an illusion.
And one time he bent
Where the elevator went
And suffered a massive contusion.
--::--

A Linotype man, problematic
Drove the machinist quite frantic.
He'd send a tight line
But most of the time
He was saved by the vise automatic.
--::--

Miss Mary the old fashioned printer,
Why printing was all she was inter.
With arms all akimbo
This robotic bimbo
Would quake from her front to her hinter!
One day while treadling her press,
A gear caught her old-fashioned dress.
As it got torn away She was heard to say
"I got caught, but I wasn't impressed!"
--::--

There once was a pressman from Bligh,
Who worked while wearing a tie.
As the cylinder turned
He suddenly learned
The effect of type meeting the eye.
--::--

A printer who worked in Des Moines

Forgot to tighten a quoin.
As the press went around
The type fell to the ground
Which he found extremely annoying.
--::--
A Printer who came from Orleans
Disdained Italic it seems.
"I really hate
That it won't stand up straight.
I'm annoyed by the way that it leans."
--::--
A printer of art in Oshgosh
Said his four-color job was a wash.
The ink went to hell
But they couldn't tell
Picasso from Hieronymus Bosch
--::--
To save rent a printer from Brewer
Set up his shop in a sewer.
He paid little rent
But the jobs that he scent
Made his customers phewer and fewer
--::--
Of course he is getting slow.
It's all that asbestos, you know.
And deadly pot fumes
In hot little rooms
It's a wonder there aint no Mo!
--::--
A printer of old worked with lead.
"It's bad for you!" it was said.
He would cry with a jeer
"I'll live many a year!
" But at age 99 he was dead.
--::--
There was a young lady from Rye
Who boiled some press parts in lye.

But she had a mishap
Some spilled in her lap
And ate away part of her thigh.
--::--
A printer from old Mandalay
Told of a most painful day.
He started to pedal
One foot under the treadle.
Now some toes will bend either way.
--::--
There once was a printer named Fred
Who had dirty rags up to his head.
With a pile that high
And the EPA guy
He now uses Kleenex instead.

My Last Hurrah
by Bob Turner

THE last hot-metal typesetting machine I ever worked on was an Intertype F4, I've still got the maker's plate!

We had to pay a scrap dealer to haul it away after I disassembled it. Sad!

This took place at Patrick & Company, a rubber stamp and marking device manufacturer at 563 Mission Street, San Francisco, California, USA, March 18-20,1987.

After this I "set" type on a Graphitec (pc/ms-dos front end, photopaper for paste-up), Compugraphic (pc/ms-dos front end, film for stripping) and a Mac+ running Ready, Set, Go! for laser paper output for rubber stamp copy.

Currently using HP state-of-the Art Laptop running Quark Express, PageMaker, Freehand and Photoshop. I've come a long way!

I first started typesetting from the case in High School. Graduated to Linotypes on the Cleveland (Ohio) News and then Intertypes on the Cleveland (Ohio) Plain Dealer. Formed a preference for the Intertypes. Chevy over Ford, Luckies over Camels, Bud over Schiitz, etc.

Also worked Cleveland (Ohio) Press, Tampa (Florida) Tribune, Clearwater (Florida) Sun, Atlanta (Georgia) Journal-Constitution and San Francisco (California) Chronicle and several small commercial shops in between.

The oldest I have run was a Model 8 Linotype and the newest was an Intertype Monarch. Went through Linotype Comets and Electrons, also the AP Linotype and I don't remember the Model No., but it was a double-plunger, 42-pica Linotype monster that brought a new dimension to the term "tight line squirt."

My favorite was a Model G4-4 Intertype with a Star Parts hydraulic quadder, a Mohr saw and split Visilite mags in 1st and 3rd position.

I am currently semi-retired (68) but working part-time at a junk-mail printer making plates for 4- and 5-color Heidelbergs, a Didde 4/1 roll-to-sheet and two Halm Jets.

I also double in brass on an MBO folder.

The Bumpy Road

by Bob Turner

HERE I sit in beautiful Dunedin, Pinellas County, Florida. 68 years old, semi-retired, working part-time for a direct mail operation where I make plates for the offset presses, run an MBO folder and bore the kids with my stories about the "good?" old days. How did I get here?

It starts with my great grandfather. He was a dabbler in printing. His son, Arthur C.Turner, my grandfather, was more than a dabbler. He started a newspaper, The West Hillsborough Times, in Clearwater, Florida, in 1884 with a few fonts and a Washington hand press. He eventually sold this equipment to some guy named R. J. Morgan who used it to start what today is the St. Petersburg (Florida) Times.

In 1893 one of his sons accompanied him to Statesboro, Georgia, my great grandfathers home town, where they established the Bulloch County Times. A. C. returned to Clearwater and the son, David (Uncle Dave) B. Turner continued to run the weekly paper until 1954. He became sort of a legend in the annals of Georgia journalism.

Another of A.C.s sons, Robert B. Turner, my father, learned printing and Linotype operation on the Clearwater Sun. My Uncle Joe did likewise. My Aunt Lillian was a proofreader at the same paper. At a young age my dad migrated to Tampa for a short time then went north to Ann Arbor, Michigan and eventually settled in Cleveland, Ohio, working on the Cleveland News. He had three kids, one of which is yours truly. During WWII he moved the family back to Clearwater and went back to work at the Clearwater Sun. I used to visit him on the job and sometimes the printers would let me play with some of the equipment. I got to feel like I was "one of the boys". After the war we went back to Cleveland and my father went back to work on the Cleveland News. My Uncle Joe stayed in Clearwater and bought his own print shop, Turner Printing, which is still in business today with my cousin, Joe, Jr. and his sons and families running the business.

Fast forward to 1952. Having been exposed to printing all my life and my becoming a printer was foreordained, I signed up for the printing class at West Tech High School in Cleveland where I honed my skills on the California Job case, the stone, the paper cutter, the C & P hand-fed, a C & P with Craftsman feeder, a Little Giant and some weird thing called a Davidson offset duplicator. In 1953 I took a part-time job after school and Saturdays as a printer's devil working on the Cleveland News with my old man. I graduated high school in 1954 and on September 13 of that year, my 18th birthday, I started my Printer's Apprenticeship on The Cleveland Plain Dealer under the auspices of The International Typographical Union, Local #53.

There were two watering holes the News guys patronized to cut the ink from their throats. The A & A at 17th and Superior, later to become the Headliner Cafe, and the Express Grill at 21st and Rockwell. The Express had its own unique identity and the Greek brothers that owned it were two such real local characters that when Dorothy Kilgallen came to town to cover the Shephard Trial for the New York Journal American, she fell in love with the place and in a column singing the praises of this "joint" declared "there's no place like this in New York City".

After two years into the Apprenticeship I "beat the draft" by signing up for four years in the U. S. Coast Guard. I also still carry U. S. Merchant Marine papers.

Back to the Plain Dealer, finished the Apprenticeship after my fifth year, got my Journeyman's Card and started my journey. It took me to the Cleveland Press, Prompt Printing, Judson Brooks Printing and Scripps Howard's NEA. After returning to the Plain Dealer I eventually became a foreman in the "Ad Alley". Left Cleveland and journeyed to Chicago for a while. The unofficial show-up room was the Ohio Inn on Ohio St., a few short blocks from the Trib, next to the Berkshire and Devonshire Hotels, the official residences of the "Tramps". Credit extended if you had a "Traveller". Then went back to Florida; the Clearwater Sun. Went to Georgia; the Atlanta Journal-Constitution. Left Atlanta and went to Flowery Branch, Georgia, to print white-page Southern Bell phone books for Georgia Ruralist Press. Back to Florida and the Tampa Tribune. Left Florida again and went to San Francisco; the San Francisco Chronicle, Bertrand's Printing, Morosi Fine Printing and Patrick & Co. The watering holes were the Tic Toc Lounge behind the Sun, the Paddock across the street from the Tampa Trib, Hanno's in the alley behind the S. F. Chron. and the S. F. Printer's Club.

Left California to go to Morganton, North Carolina to help my brother set up a quick-copy and printing brokerage business. After six years took a job as night manager of a Sir Speedy shop in Charlotte, North Carolina. After six years – six months after my 66th birthday I quit and came back to Florida.

In between some of these printing jobs I found time to pursue other paths. Sailor, charter fishing guide, car salesman, bum. All these paths lead right back to my present semi-retired, part-time employment in a cutting-edge direct-mail operation printing "junk mail". One man's trash (garbage), another man's treasure (gold). I have seen it all; from hand-set to Linotype to phototype to laser type. Letterpress to offset to flexo. Lead, rubber, photopolymer plastic and aluminium plates. Or no plates. In addition to our offset presses at the junk-mail shop, we also have six high-speed black and white laser printers and the latest Xerox that prints 12×18 in full color, two sides, with bleeds and variable graphics and text on each impression, all at or near press speeds. Everything is produced and printed from digital files.

I've had to roll with some punches, adapt to some far-out technology, bend with the force of change over a lifetime in printing. It was and still is a bumpy, rough, wonderful ride and I wouldn't hesitate doing it all over again if I could. I can't wait to see what's coming down the pipeline next. In the mean time, I've been there, done that, and probably printed the T-shirt.

Taken on at Spicers

by Roy Bowker

SO WHERE do I start? Well my first insight to the printing game was at secondary modern school when the teacher asked if anybody was interested in joining a printing class that was being started. My hand went up basically because a friend of mine had volunteered.

Come the time to leave school and having written to umpteen numbers of printers, in and around London, I was still without any firm offer of work. The one firm that I did get a little bit of joy from was "Ede and Townsend" who were near Finsbury Square I think.

They had said in a reply that there may be a vacancy in the composing room and would let me know at a later date. So off I went to my scout's summer camp hoping that when I came back I would be in the trade. However the letter that was waiting for me gave some excuse which I cannot remember, all I do know is that there was no job for me.

One of my uncles was in the trade; in fact he was an overseer at Spicers in Union Street just over Blackfriars Bridge. My parents did not really want me to ask him to try and get me in at Spicers as they thought "they would always be beholden to him and that he would not let them forget it" in actual fact I never found uncle Fred anything like that, but maybe my parents knew different.

In the end however my parents said go ahead and ask Fred if there was any chance of a vacancy in any department at Spicers. By this time I had written to almost every printer in and around London, so I guess they thought there was no alternative.

Whilst I was waiting for a positive answer from Fred or Spicers, I got a job at a piano factory that my father had worked in before he started working for himself as a French polisher. I was only there for two weeks when I got the necessary letter I had been waiting for, an interview with the personnel officer at Spicers. The interview went well and I think I started work about the following Monday in the printing machine dept.

Apprentice "Banging In"

I know that various print houses in and around London had their own traditions/quirks but I believe that Spicers to be the only firm that used to "bang in" their apprentices. This I was soon to find out, much to my detriment!

I remember it was a Friday; my apprenticeship papers had been signed in the presence of the personnel officer (Miss Faulk), my Mother, Mr. Arthur Jenkins (who was my very good mentor) and myself. After the signing I went back to my department. What happened about an hour later back in the print room took me completely by surprise. My cousin who worked in Uncle Fred's department (a different dept. to mine) came over to me, grabbed me around the waist and with the help of somebody else in the shop tied my hands over the top of a pulley shaft! (Not a lot of health and safety in 1954) and my feet were on one of the work benches. Then the next thing, yes you've guessed it, my trousers and underpants were pulled down! The male members of my dept then proceeded to smear "bronze blue" around my parts.

These actions by themselves would have been a laugh but, the fact that there were women present and young ones at that brought real tears to my eyes. On top of this humiliation I was left there for over an hour, and during that time it got around the factory that I was there in all my glory and all the other departments came to see, and believe me Spicers was a very big building with lots of departments and employees.

Well that's the account of my "banging in", I would like to know if any other firm has or had the same kind of thing?

I have seen many "banging outs" since then, but somehow its not the same as being on the receiving end of a gloved hand full of the dreaded bronze blue. Oh and by the way, it's nearly all scrubbed off now!

The Proofreader's Nighrmare
by Frank Granger

all the sentences started with lower case.
The 3 em indent was way two much space.
The Futuria type was very, very bold,
Also not the face the customer was sold.
Of linespacing theree was plenty.
Who'd ever heard of ten on twenty.
From the word shirt they dropped a letter.
She would tell you, it could be be better.
The ink was green – it should have been red,
"Here's another P.E.." someone said.
There were more typos here than one could guess.
Oh, how did it ever get to press?
A million impressions? Already delivered?
And still more mistakes. She only quivered.
Maybe. It was someone else's goof?
No, her were here initials righ on the proof.
The proofreader awoke, and set up in bed!
Ouch! What a feeling she had in her head!
But what a relief, it was only a dream,
And from now on, no more pickles and ice cream.

Note: This poem is full of intentional Printer's Errors or "P.E.'s." Educators might present this to a proofreading class to see if the students can catch all the mistakes.

The New Apprentice in 1904
by Frank Granger

I like this printing job I just got.
But there are things I wish were not.
For example, some task assigned just today
Were useless work, I'd hazard to say.
"A paper stretcher!" the pressman did call,
"You might find one over by the wall."
I looked and looked, but couldn't find it.
Later he said to never-mind it!
But the engraver needed some halftone dots,
And by the paper drill I found lots and lots!
The Linotype man was very concerned.
He had a serious problem, I later learned.
The type lice had invaded our shop
And I was sent out and told not to stop.
Until I had warned every printer near,
Which I did and then came right back here.
I got back just a little bit after lunch
A little too late, I had a hunch.
Because the "pie" they said I could clean up
Was all gone and all I got was to pick-up
Some jumbled type spilled on the floor.
It was a tedious job and quite a bore.
When I went for the poke-a-dot ink,
I thought I saw the foreman wink.
At the guy needing the left-hand wrench,
Which was supposed to be at the bindery bench.
Yes, they sure keep me on the run,
But, I don't mind since I am having fun,
And our shop is a right friendly place.
When I come in there's a smile on every face.

Note: Good-natured tricks were commonly played on the novice printers. Paper stretchers and halftone dots were common. Type that was not cast at the right temperature had tiny pinholes and type lice were blamed. A printer's "pi" was a jumble of type. Pi Sheng was the first inventor of printing in China over a thousand years before Gutenberg. It is thought that printers honored Pi by naming odd type characters and jumbled letters after him.

Elrod Memories

by Dan Williams

ANY PRINT SHOP of the letterpress era needed loads of spacing material. My dad's type shop was no exception.

His name was Eugene Williams and he operated his commercial type shop on Mayfair Boulevard, Houston, Texas from the mid 1950s until he died in 1985.

I recall those occasional weekend trips to the family shop where so many sweep-up, piglet hauling and other tasks were assigned to my young hands. From my earliest memory of those weekend trips, dad produced spacing material using an old, torn-down composition caster.

Sometime during my grammar school years, I recall our procuring a replacement for this old caster. The "new" machine was an Elrod. I regarded this Elrod as a very odd mechanism not so much for its impossibly top-heavy appearance (from a child's eye-view), but more for the mysterious attention it seemed to draw from the extended family and customers. "Casts bulk 18 and 24 point" I recall hearing.

This brought form to an interesting childhood experience. On that Saturday of the Elrod inauguration, I had left the shop for a brief playground visit. On my return, I could sense commotion. From somewhere in that shop, deep far back, there was a cacophony. Mechanical and verbal excitement.

Gathering some courage, I forced myself inside to see the action. Peering around the brick, I gasped at the scene: impressive bursts of steam, bursts of molten lead and smoke shooting out from the monstrosity's gut.

Thankfully, my father stood clear. In that corner behind the Elrod flywheel, I could see him one-arm wrestle the big pump handle, slapping the lower control panel (I speculate now, for the switch) with his other free hand. Looking rather serious and intent, he caught my eye, hand-motioned wildly with one newly-silvered glove, and in my general direction loudly uttered something very direct, yet completely unintelligible. Who was going to win the battle? I could not bear to see. I ran out of the building and hid outside, hoping dad could eventually fight his way out. Thankfully I was not disappointed, for my father soon emerged, apologized for the confusion, and thanked me for leaving the machine. He stammered something about a stuck pin or lost mold.

I do not recall a similar problem ever again. The Elrod was frequently used, producing such prolific quantities of spacing material that for a short time, it became a saleable commodity for the family business.

Eventually I overcame my fear of the machine. By the time I was a senior in high school, I was sufficiently competent that I could pull 2 pt strip on the first try. My last visual memory of our Elrod was my having to pull it, with comealong and pipes, out of the building (now estate property), leaving it near the street for nightly "junk elves" to pick up.

Technology and human life cycle being its demise.

A World of Type
by Steve Young

I STARTED my working life at the Hampshire Chronicle in 1965 as an apprentice comp, but very soon graduated on to the line and to my own refurbished Model 4.

I called it "The Dream" - I eventually learned to clear the 3ft. copy box to my right in one easy bound when I heard the distinctive "clunk" whenever the line misplaced in the jaws and hot metal shot out through the bent mat. Many times I didn't make it and still have those scars we all know about down my left leg. My Times (D7) 7pt (ruby) font suffered badly.

Left Winchester when I came out of my time in 1970 and went to work as a Lino Op on the Diamond Fields Advertiser in Kimberley, South Africa – trebled my wage immediately and had the time of my life for three years before relocating within the Argus company up to the Rhodesia Herald in Salisbury working the night shift on American Blue Streak and Comet machines plus a couple of C4s and a couple of side magazine 78s for ads! Rhodesia was a lovely and beautiful country, Happy days, it's truly disastrous what has occurred there over the last 20 years or so!

Anyway ... I went back down to SA in 1976 to The Natal Witness operating Lino 78s and 48s and then finally transferred to Hendrix computer setting in 1977. Working the line for magazines in the morning and the system in the afternoon on the newspaper.

Back to the UK in 1977 and up to Stoke to a position running the old Universal 4, Edit Writer and MSC Compugraphic systems as Systems Manager ... and when that hid the skids in 84 I got a position with

Crosfield Hastech (the old Hendrix vendor) installing new generation systems as the computer revolution took hold of the industry ... if you can't beat 'em join 'em is my philosophy. Worked at the Liverpool Post and Echo on their upgrade and supported Today newspaper after Eddie Shah sold it on.

Since then I have worked with a variety of systems vendors right around the world (Du Pont, PPI, Unisys) from Australia, New Zealand, the US, throughout Europe and of course the UK, selling, installing, supporting and trouble shooting the latest generation of front end systems. I spent 6 months commuting to/from San Francisco for the SF Chronicle and stayed in Boston for thee months with the Boston Herald installation as well as up to Wisconsin in the dead of winter to the wastes of Waupaca in 1999. The longest install I was involved with was at El Correo Espagnol in Bilbao and Diario de Vasco in San Sebastian was back in 1989 — also a "revolutionary" system being the first SQL database with which I was involved.

I spent about 9 months at the British Medical Journal in London installing their new system and am about to go back in there for the last knockings of the phase 2 part of the install — luckily I was over in east London at another newspaper when the bus exploded right outside my BMJ office.

I guess I have been doubly lucky in that regard as I left New York on 9/10 to run a presentation in Dublin at the Irish Independent on that tragic day in 2001 ... needless to say the presentation finished very early and I took my American colleagues back to London as of course there was no flights back to the US for a week or so.

However, I was made redundant from Unisys soon after then with 3000 others as the company experienced a massive downturn in business as a direct result of that tragedy. I worked for Atex for three months in New York before gaining a similar position in the UK and have spent the last three years or so working at newspapers and magazines here in the British Isles.

At 57 years old I am about to get off the road and semi-retire to my house in France.

But I don't think the current generation of newspaper professionals know what it's like to work in the newsroom on a morning paper when all the machines were at full stretch, running up to 15 lines a minute to get the paper off stone — it was an experience. I loved it and will miss being involved in and around newspapers and those involved with them for the rest of my life.

Casting Ingots
by Les Smith

HOT METAL shops were great recyclers of type metal and usually hidden in a less attractive location would be the equipment to melt the metal, skim off the dross and cast the ingots.

Typically the metal was cast into a cast iron mould with a water jacket to cool the mould, ingots and stop the iron cracking. The one I remember had multiple recesses to enable four ingots to be cast at a time. It was fed from a gas heated vat that looked not unlike grandma's clothes copper.

The mould was set up to pivot so when the metal had set, the mould would be tipped and the ingots dumped into a bin. Open on top with little regard for the atmosphere. In summer a large fan provided token relief of the operator.

The casting operation worked six days a week. This particular Saturday morning one of the managers decided to help pour the first ingots of the day. Given the way the business operated all the new starters had the opportunity to do the dirty jobs. And this manager was no different, having worked his way up he did know how to pour ingots.

The metal was at the correct temperature, fuming nicely as it did. Fill the first mould, then the second, the third and then with the fourth all hell broke loose. The modern Australian vernacular goes something like, the brown stuff has hit the Mistral. In this case it was the white stuff had hit the water! Metal all over the place.

The cast iron mould after years of use, had cracked ever so slightly and water from the cooling jacket would seep into the mould. If the water tap was left on overnight with the mould the right way up, a little would accumulate, just to catch the unwary.

Regular operators were aware of this quirk and would tip the mould before the first pour of the day. Our helpful manager wasn't aware of these later developments and one might say was caught red faced.

Fortunately no one was injured with the lead spitting out of the mould until the water boiled off!!!

Apparently the reception at home was a complete contrast, rather frosty when time came to explain the destroyed pair of very good suit pants.

Wonder what Workcover, OH&S and the Union would have to say about such an apparatus these days. Somehow I think I know ...

The Apprentice's Printer's Pie
by Mike Wilson

MIKE SAID: "I'm writing tales in poetry about my childhood. And as I looked at your site today I seem to think I saw the words "Printer's Pie." So I sat and composed this poem. It's a blank verse sonnet, which the writers tell me is difficult to do. But this one just fell into place. Hope you like it.

The blokes at work made me a pie today.
They wrapped it up with strong and sturdy string.
It seemed too heavy to be a normal pie
but they said the pie would go with anything.
I took it home and gave it to my mum
She smiled when told who'd given it to me
"We'll have it for our tea tonight then, son,
" and hid the pie. She wouldn't let me see.
When teatime came I loved the apple pie;
with custard made by Mum, it tasted good.
My portion seemed to have no weight at all
but I was pleased to eat their printer's pud.
They laughed at me next day. I wondered why.
They told me what is really printer's pie.

Wayzgoose –The Event of the Year
by G G Whyman

HE was one of the last of the old tramp compositors-cum-linotype operators-cum printers. Once upon a time they were a numerous tribe; today they are as outdated as movable type in newspaper headings.

Unerringly he approached the traditional enemy of his kind. "You want a compositor," he said, telling the printer, rather than asking him. "We've got one." "You want a machinist," he demanded. "We've got one." "Then," he asserted, with the desperation of one who simply must have work, however lowly, "d'you want an editor?"

That story has raised many a laugh where newspaper types gather and inevitably talk shop. It is not apocryphal. It was an actual happening in a small newspaper office in the back country of New South Wales and was told to me by one of the nomadic tribe of compositors who after worldwide experience became one of the Weekly News staff.

Confidence

THESE old tramps would walk into print shops or newspaper offices with a quiet confidence – almost an arrogance – born from the knowledge that they were journeymen in every sense of the word, that they were as good at their craft as man could be.

They took offence easily, many of them; they were as proud of their skills as hawks. And they could drink. Indeed yes ...

One such character appeared before the printer of the Weekly News one morning, not long after the turn of the century. He wore a shirt, pants and shoes without socks. He and the demon drink were obviously bedfellows. The bloom of the hop blossoms was apparent on his cheeks and nose.

He said he was a linotype operator. Such a linotype operator as never was seen setting type in all the colonies. In other words, he was good. He has come ashore from the San Francisco mail packet a few days previously, nattily attired, with money in his pocket, had fallen into bad company, been "rolled" of money and clothes by his drinking companions, missed his boat to Australia, and he needed a job. He talked himself into one.

And while all the nine other operators who comprised the total mechanical typesetting staff of the Weekly News of the time peered round corners and marveled at the shower of flashing brass matrices which fell and assembled at such wizard fingering as they had never dreamed of, no one thought it even passing strange that the copy which was being set into type by the tramp was the weekly sermon, without which no respectable paper ever went to press, or that the subject of this particular sermon dealt with the "Evils of Alcoholic Liquor."

Anthology

THIS nomad brought with him an anthology of newspaper stories. He swore that he had worked on the small-town Mississippi State Journal which had published prematurely the death notice and obituary of one of the town's most prominent citizens. The editor had heard the news less than an hour before the paper was put to bed.

Actually he committed one of the cardinal sins of journalism – he had not checked the story. But he still ran it. And while he may not have been one half of a duel the next morning, he was threatened with a horse-whipping, one of the more favoured forms of public humiliation in the State, and it was demanded by the irate and very-much-alive object of the obituary notice, that a retraction of the news and an apology be published in the next week's issue.

The editor was adamant. The published word can never be retracted, he said. Nor would he admit that his journal had made a mistake. But with a buggy-whip being flourished within inches of his imperial purple nose he agreed that the paper would make some form of amends. It did.

A week later, beneath the heading "Births and Deaths" there appeared the following: "Strathcombe, Ezra Jacob. Died October 2, 1901; reborn October 9, 1901." On being given a job on the Weekly News of those days this character has achieved something which previously was thought to be impossible without the aid of dynamite. With maybe one exception, the staff had learned their trade from the journeymen before them and they were jealous of their reputations as craftsmen and of the reputation of the paper on which they worked.

Entree

TO have been a journeyman on the Weekly News was to have entree to any paper in the world, it was said. And the old-timers believed that, just as they believed that their paper was published every Wednesday and come hell or high water, their paper would be on the streets because the public, the subscribers, believed it would be on the streets every Wednesday.

These were men who, like generations before them, had been indentured apprentices to the craft of typesetting by hand – before Ottmar Mergenthaler produced his first linotype, the mechanical typesetter which revolutionised the newspaper industry.

As apprentices they were taught the "trade and business; they were provided with good and sufficient diet, lodging, washing, medicine and all other necessaries fit for an apprentice" and they were even paid a few shillings a week. In return they worked 48 hours a week, contracting not to enter (presumably the greatest of all evils) "matrimony, nor embezzle, waste or lend, or play at cards or other unlawful games or bet or haunt or frequent public houses or taverns but in all things demean himself as a good and faithful apprentice ought to do."

A boy's first confusing weeks in a newspaper office. The cases of type – the Bodonis, the Goudy, the Scripts, the Gothics, the Caslons, the infinite varieties of the Cheltenham workhorses. The very terms: the quoins, the footsticks, the quadrants. And the smell! Ink, paper, that witches' brew lye, and above all, dirt. Windowsills deep in dust, dead bugs and occasional old letters of type. Many a printer's devil believed that purgatory could never be so grim as a composing room.

Until comparatively recent times the Weekly News employed three apprentices. And three only. They held copy for the readers, they swept floors, they cleaned lavatories, they gave cheek, they were clipped on the ears (sometimes over the other end), they thought the journeymen were next to God, they learned that the printer was God.

And gradually they also learned "the case," that jigsaw contraption in which movable type was contained, by "dissing," or distributing used types. Inevitably as "devils" they made the acquaintance of the "hell box," that satin-inspired punishment for unruly boys, wherein was thrown every ill-assorted letter, space, rule, every adjunct of a compositor's craft which had strayed from its case into the "hell box" awaiting distribution.

Pieceworkers

HE learned his craft – and its traditions. And he became proud of both. Even as an apprentice he served part of his six years "time" on night shift among those superior beings the pieceworkers, setting the New Zealand Herald by hand. Every good boy aspired to become a pieceworker – some day.

But before then he remained, as an apprentice, one of the lowest forms of life inhabiting a newspaper office. It is told that one of the duties of the night shift apprentice in the hand-setting days was to take a billy (about the size of a milking bucket) to the Metropolitan Hotel, 50 yards from the office, where it was filled with beer, (for 1 shilling) for the comps' supper.

It was well-established practice until one very naive youth "spilt the beans" to his parents that the previous night – his first on night shift – one chore had been to visit the Met.

It was a breach of his indentures, they proclaimed. Furthermore, the boy was under age. Furthermore, what sort of men would send an innocent youth into a hotel at night?

An innocent youth? In a newspaper office? The protest sparked off a fine how-d'ye-do. There was no talk of strike, or even an insurrection. Actually, the story today has no ending. But one thing was sure: the compositors would have their beer!

Journeyman

BUT eventually all good things come to an end. Even a six-year apprenticeship. And the newly fledged journeyman, admitted to the companionship of the chapel – that embryo union, so-named because Caxton set up the first printing works in a chapel of Westminster Abbey – if he was both lucky and good enough, would be allocated a "frame," usually by flickering gaslight and a few inches of candle, and he became a pieceworker, handpicking type for the news columns of the New Zealand Herald and Weekly News.

Or he became a grasshand. To be a "grassy" was an ideal occupation for a young single man. Particularly in summer. He would appear in the office in the early afternoon and if a permanent employee was to absent himself for a night's work, his "frame" went to the first grasshand available. Otherwise he was "turned out to grass" for that day and night.

One old "grassy" told me that for four years he wanted nothing better. He would get three to four nights a week, earn maybe 3 pounds, and wouldn't call the king his uncle. Particularly when he could go swimming or pulling a whaleboat for the Auckland Rowing Club in the afternoons. And then a girl. Finis.

"Dissing"

FORTY-EIGHT hours a week newspaper hands worked in those days. But the 48 hours did not include the couple of hours spent every afternoon "dissing" the type of the previous night's paper. Under the jurisdiction of the Father of the Chapel all type was evenly and fairly distributed among the pieceworkers and it was their responsibility – indeed a necessity to fill their cases for the coming night's work. They worked hard and they played hard.

They started work at 6 p.m. They finished when the paper went to press, be it 3 a.m., 4 a.m., or 5 a.m. It is even on record that after the introduction of linotypes the "higher-ups" planned to introduce double-column introductions to one or two stories. At seven a.m. the introductions still had not been set – no operator had ever set such a long line of type mechanically without a literal error. The story goes that the first attempt was given up in disgust at 7.30 a.m.

The first linotypes came to the Weekly News before 1900. They were the objects of derision here as they had been overseas. But when several hand compositors were given the opportunity to operate the new wonders they accepted with alacrity. And thereby they joined the ranks of the "piano players," as the scoffers and the Jeremiahs dubbed them.

"To think that such heaps of junk will replace hand compositors!" they said. "They'll be thrown out in six months and you fellows will be looking for jobs." But that is another story ... even if it does appear that the days of the linotype are about to be numbered in metropolitan newspaper offices. Linotypes made possible the production of bigger papers in a shorter time. They made composing cleaner, perhaps less injurious to health, perhaps they made the work easier.

At any rate they could not have influenced their operators to play any easier. For, as with their hand setting forebears, their day of the year was the annual "wayzgoose."

Peculiarly a printer's excuse for a beanfeast – as if printers and their minions ever needed an excuse for a beanfeast! - the wayzgoose has been brought from England when the colony was settled.

In the Old land it had been celebrated usually about August 24, the excuse being that with the advent of winter and the failing of natural light, the masters were required to provide their compositors with an extra inch or two more of candle by which to set type.

Celebration

SUCH magnanimity called for celebration – at the master's expense of course – and thereby there came into being the annual wazgoose at which the piece de resistance was roast goose – also provided at the master's expense. Washed down with olde English ale, of course.

Well, in New Zealand the goose was dispensed with. And instead of holding their annual wayzgoose in August the Weekly News newsroom staffs and the editorial staff held their wayzgoose annually in January, sometimes in February. It was usually hotter weather for the object of the exercise.

In horsedrawn brakes they journeyed to Howick, 12 miles from Auckland, through the green farmlands of those days. Now Howick is a city. But for the purpose of a wayzgoose 60, 70, 80 years ago it was ideal. There was a store, a post office, an Oddfellow's Hall, a paddock for athletic exercises – and there was a pub.

Even more popular was Riverhead, ideally situated at the head of the Waitemata Harbour. There was a paddock – and there, too, was the welcoming entrance of the Foresters Arms.

Almost 60 years ago the highlight of virtually the last Weekly News wayzgoose held at Riverhead could still raise a chuckle from one of the hand comps who had been present. And, I suspect, a participant.

By way of the Eden Vine, the Stone Jug and the Haupai Hotel the Weekly News brake arrived at Riverhead, only to find that their paddock had been invaded by the Sunday School picnic of a church which still flourishes today.

Undaunted, and knowing that not all the revellers would be on the paddock at the same time, they took over a small corner, both parties treating that other with strict ignore.

The highlight of the wayzgoose was the greasy pig competition. Not only had the poor beast been literally dabbed with grease, but also some alleged wit had painted on his flanks the words "wrong fount," meaning a size of type of particular face which had strayed from its fellows and was due to find its way into the "hell box."

Never was a pig, greasy or otherwise, more aptly named. He was released seconds before the padre clapped his hands together to start the single ladies, race, run over a distance of 75 yards, for no purse at all. And while the junior student' lolly scramble was in progress too.

Possibly seeking ecclesiastical sanctuary, Wrong Fount took off. He upset the single ladies when in full cry and the others in the field became surrounded with

Whirling Dervishes from the wayzgoose. The lolly scramble disintegrated and Wrong Font was swimming furiously in the direction of South America.

Australian Linotype Mechanic
by George Finn

IN APRIL 1948, when I was 15, my brother, who was a compositor at The Wagga Daily Advertiser, in New South Wales, got me a job as office boy. After six months I was indentured to serve a six year apprenticeship, as a Linotype Mechanic.

At that time the paper had a battery of ten Linotypes, a Ludlow and an Elrod machine.

The first day on the job as an apprentice, I was helping move a Linotype from the newspaper to the job printing department. As we moved the machine off the concrete base, it fell straight through the wooden floor, to the ground two feet below. The distributor hit me on the shoulder and sent me flying behind the next machine. The mechanic said "Oh my God, look at the machine!" An old Linotype operator looking on said "Bugger the machine. Where's the Boy?"

The Boy was "OK" and got lots of experience helping rebuild the machine, after the broken parts were welded and the bent parts straightened. Fortunately there were a couple of good fitter-welders there.

I finished my apprenticeship and worked at The Advertiser for a couple of years as a tradesman.

We had a comp working with us from Launceston Tasmania. He was the first person I saw who could water-ski barefoot.

Anyhow he went back to Tassie to work at the Launceston Examiner. He wrote me a letter using the Examiner's stationery. I was on night work at the time, and the letter was posted on a notice board where mail and such were left for the night staff.

When I collected the letter there was also note from the Advertiser's General Manager, asking if I would come and see him the next day.

The letter was asking a favour and was of no consequence, except that when I saw the GM, he asked me if I'd like a transfer to the Sydney Morning Herald.

The GM of the SMH was part owner of the Wagga Advertiser. I said "Sure I'd love to." He said "Good I'll make the arrangements. You'll be better off there than in Launceston!"

This goes to prove, "You can't judge a letter by the envelope!"

The Glass Door

by Don Hauser

FROM age ten I remember messing about with my John Bull Printing Outfit and a cocktail of glycerine, gelatine, builders' glue, methylated spirits and violet hectograph ink, the basics of a primitive spirit duplicator as prescribed in Hobbies Illustrated circa 1949.

In grade five at Tyler Street primary school, Preston, my first newspaper, The Weekly Trumpet, was hand lettered on quarto paper and pinned to the class notice board. About this time my mother bought her first washing machine, a Hoover with a fold-away hand-wringer. "What a perfect way to run off a few copies of the Trumpet and sell them to the kids" I thought! But something went terribly wrong. Instead of the violet hectograph-inked paper-master soaked in methylated spirits transferring onto white paper, it ended up on the wringers of mother's new pride and joy! The Weekly Trumpet appeared on whites and coloureds for weeks until the image disappeared.

At Northcote Boys' High School in form 2c I began the Two Cee Gazette a hand-written and illustrated paper that appeared on the form notice-board. John Daniel, another boy in the same form, started a rival 2c Star. Mr Dean, our English master of the day, (known to the boys as "Clipper" for his frequent clipping of young ears) spotted the educational benefit and suggested "a merger". The result was the Associated Newspapers Magazine. We were allowed restricted use of the school's Gestetner duplicator and Banda spirit duplicator; now we could print supplements and feature pages in living colour! John Daniel and I alternated as editor and deputy editor. The paper continued but while I was in form three my father died after a long illness. Our family moved to Surrey Hills and I was sent to Camberwell High School. My new co-educational school environment failed to interest me on any level. I was a sorry lad and wished to conclude my schooling.

My mother, widowed and apprehensive, gave me her permission to leave Camberwell High School and find an apprenticeship in printing.

Arthur L. Edgerton, printers and envelope makers of City Road, South Melbourne employed me on probation as an apprentice hand-compositor. Edgertons specialised in producing envelopes of every description! I soon discovered that six years of hand setting "if not claimed within seven days, please return to" was not my idea of typographical skill! Furthermore, I didn't endear myself to my employer when ink remover that I was using to clean varnish off a Heidelberg platen press (varnish used to print the translucent windows on envelopes) leaked through the floorboards onto a brand new red Chevrolet Bel Air sedan in the workshop below. A shiny metallic hole appeared through several layers of new enamel paintwork.

Robert Schurmann ran a commercial art studio in Swan Street, Richmond. He prepared finished artwork for retail advertisements for newspapers using photographic bromide prints and typeset patches from type he stored in matchbox trays and proofed on a small Adana hand press. He also taught typographical design part-time at the Melbourne School of Printing and Graphic Arts then located at Melbourne Technical College, building number 4 in Bowen Street. He learned that I was looking for an apprenticeship and arranged for me to visit Exchange Press in Spencer Street for an interview.

Exchange Press

I started there, again on probation, with apprenticeship in view. The pay was three pounds, two shillings and sixpence per week with a five shilling increase in my first apprentice year. My new-found skill in typesetting if not claimed etc. in size eight point meant that I could easily set up my first job, a wedding invitation ... Mr & Mrs Brown request the pleasure of the company of etc. ... in size twelve point wedding text without requiring any tuition.

Bill Hewitt, a tall distinguished looking man was the composing room foreman with excellent teaching skills and outstanding ability as a typographer and designer. Bill Hewitt was a father figure to me and I believe that he recognised this and gladly passed on his many skills for my benefit.

Archie Campbell was a fine compositor and linotype operator. On my first day, he advised me to leave my lunch high on a shelf to avoid having it mauled by rats - on the same shelf as the weeks old milk in glass bottles. From that day to this, my tea has remained black.

Subsequently, I became an indentured apprentice, bound to Exchange Press at 263 Spencer Street, Melbourne. On 31 October, 1952, J. H. (Alan) Eaton, managing director, John Bennett, company secretary, my mother Isobel and I were in attendance to sign my indentures. The term was six years and at the age of fourteen and a half, this seemed to me like the term of my natural life. I had become an apprentice hand and machine (linotype) compositor.

From day one it was abundantly clear to me that the junior apprentice (or worse, the provisional junior apprentice), got the "shit jobs" until such time that one was replaced by someone who was more junior.

Sweeping the composing room floor, cleaning the two pot-bellied stoves and setting their fires in the winter, getting the lunches, making the tea in a grubby aluminium teapot; this was all first year apprentice work. We were told that this work was "character building". Linotype metal was recycled by melting the used lead in a gas fired "metal pot" in a grubby corrugated iron shed in the backyard. The metal was then ladled into ingot shaped moulds. During a downpour, rain leaked through holes in the roof into the molten lead filled crucible spattering lead over my dustcoat and face if I wasn't careful. I felt akin to 500 years of printers' devils.

Any chance to learn was always interrupted by being sent on messages all over town. Pick up some type, run down to Hudson's Stores in Bourke Street for a tube of glue, deliver a proof to the always dapper Alf Cheel at the Claude Mooney Advertising agency in the Temple Court building in Collins Street.

Once a month, I was given the union dues in a bag and sixpence for tram fares to take to the Printing and Allied Trades Employees Union in the Trades Hall. Of course I pocketed the fare and ran like fury through the Flagstaff Gardens and down Franklin Street to Lygon Street, up the stairs to the first floor almost collapsing from exhaustion. The kindly Ernie Heintz (father of Alby Heintz) sat me down with a cup of black tea before the return sprint.

Getting the lunches involved crossing Spencer Street and taking a deep breath passing the smelly hide and skin store on the corner of Spencer and Little Lon. (now the site of the Age editorial department) and walking the block to the lunch shop in King Street. My senior colleague John Grainger quite enjoyed a midday walk in the fresh air and agreed to share the task on alternate days.

As time progressed I became more proficient at hand setting lead type from dusty typecases or drawers into a composing "stick" or hand-held tray; handsetting matrices and casting lines of lead display type in a Ludlow Typograph. Later, I was let loose on Ottmar

Mergenthaler's previously mentioned amazing Linotype machine. Invented in 1884, this machine completely revolutionised the typesetting of newspapers, books and journals. A fast operator could keyboard ten newspaper ten em column lines per minute. Never having had time to practise on only one available machine, I suppose that I achieved no more than about four lines a minute.

The personnel at Exchange Press were a good crew. They consisted mainly of journeymen printers, compositors and an assortment of bindery ladies, travellers and office workers. To a young apprentice, they were a source of learning and fun.

Henry Cole, white-haired, quiet and stooped from years working a paper cutter, taught me about paper types and sizes and showed me how to fan-out and count sheets by fives.

Production manager Norm Hilliard once played Australian Football for Fitzroy when they were called the Maroons. Les (Wacker) Wells ran the despatch department. A Fitzroy stalwart, Wacker served the oranges at quarter and three-quarter time every Saturday.

Eddie Wittenberg, an immigrant from war torn Hungary, joined the firm briefly as a hand compositor/linotype operator. Eddie later bought into and developed a small printer called Abaris Printing. Today Abaris is the last of Melbourne's large printers and will soon move to the western suburbs. Bertie Bridgeland set up his chair next to his Kelly printing press to provide lunchtime haircuts for "a bob" (a shilling or ten cents). The managing director was a regular customer.

During the composing apprenticeship, we worked with lead type, lead and wood spacing covered in lead dust and stereotypes made of lead. Whether the long term ingestion of lead is attributable to my average state of health will never be known. However it was never my plan to remain "on the bench" as a journeyman compositor. I moved on to a new position the day after my indentures expired. A little thoughtless I considered in retrospect.

Gold bronzing meant dusting powdered bronze powder to sheets printed with a tacky slow drying ink. The dust drifted everywhere into eyes, clothes and ingested into lungs. One would be given money to buy a half pint of milk apparently to absorb the dreaded dust and line ones stomach and gut.

Learning a trade always involved observing, listening, trying out new skills, studying and having the manual and mental dexterity to skilfully handle materials, equipment, machinery and respect raw and sometimes dangerous materials.

Melbourne School of Printing and Graphic Arts

The first contact I had with the Melbourne School of Printing and Graphic Arts as it was then known, was at an interview in September, 1951 with Wally Wolsenholm who taught English and maths at the old school building in Queensberry Street, North Melbourne. The purpose of the interview was to establish that I was a suitable candidate for apprenticeship to Exchange Press.

The following year I began day school, a half day per fortnight plus two nights a week, at Melbourne Technical College, Bowen Street (off Latrobe Street), until 1945 known as the Working Mens' College. I trudged the well-worn staircase in the old Gothic building No. 4 for three years until the letterpress printing department moved to the new building in Queensberry Street, North Melbourne.

Frank Matthias was the head of the letterpress department at Bowen Street and James E. (Jim) Turney, the senior composing instructor. Frank Woodlock taught science, maths and English; Percy Ludgate,

Monotype keyboard and caster. At night school, Frank Campbell, a wartime airman, taught typographical design. He was assisted part time by Bob Schurmann.

For the first half of my first year, I was far from being a high achiever. I recall a test result of 17 per cent for maths. Following a very strong pep talk from Mr Woodlock, I improved my end of year mark for maths to 97 per cent and went on to take overall first prize for first, second and third years. In addition, I earned several prizes and bronze medallions for scholastic and craftsmanship awards. In 1959, I was awarded a Victorian Overseas Foundation travelling scholarship which provided the opportunity to gain work experience in USA and England for two and a half years. To my sorrow, Frank Woodlock died before I ever considered or found the opportunity to thank him for his trust in my ability to improve and succeed.

In 1956, the letterpress department moved from Bowen Street to the new building located behind the original state school in Queensberry Street, North Melbourne. The building was officially opened by the Governor of Victoria, Sir Dallas Brooks on Thursday, 27 March, 1958. I continued my apprenticeship studies at North Melbourne as a linotype operator with Gordon Castle and later completed advanced courses at the college.

The Glass Door

A key plank of Jim Turney's tuition was, at least for his more aspiring students, to progress to somewhere "behind the glass door" distanced from the lead, the machinery and the noise to a collar and tie job in typographical design, sales, planning and estimating or general management. Turney, a skilled compositor, served his apprenticeship with Osboldstone & Co. prior to his appointment as a technical teacher in 1937. His accomplishments as a teacher, his strong character, his friendship and his dry humour are remembered by many hundreds of his students. Jim's retirement was marked at a dinner arranged by past and present students at Menzies Hotel on 30 September, 1968.

The school principal, John Lodge, came from the English Midlands and was well qualified to head a printing educational institution. He was assisted by department heads, Bill Brown, Jim Turney, Bill Glasson and Ray Stratford. John Lodge and his senior staff played a very large part in planning and re-equipping the new school in Queensberry Street with the latest technology of the day. Clearly, the MSP&GA was then the best equipped polytechnic printing school in the world. As a student there, I deemed it a privilege.

Returning from overseas, I worked for a year with the D. W. Paterson Company as a film make up compositor. Newly married to Jill Wilson whom I met in London, I joined the production department of USP Benson Advertising and later, with Jackson Wain Advertising as production manager for five years.

Opportunity knocks and another leaf in the book

Opportunity knocked when my job was terminated after Jackson Wain was acquired by Leo Burnett Advertising of Chicago. By March 1971, I commenced work as a printing consultant in a shared office at 564 St. Kilda Road. With a supportive partner, three children, a mortgage plus the accompanying business expenses there were a few worrying months but the decision to risk everything paid off.

We moved to rented premises in Jolimont in 1975 and purchased our own property in 1982. John Naismith, Peter Campbell, Julie Perium, Jane Stokie, Melinda Traves, Helen Grieve, Megan O'Neil, Graham Radford, Debbie Friedrich, my wife Jill and daughter Amanda all worked here over a period of time. We were a part of a small family business helping to service some blue ribbon customers including ANZ Bank, Australian Dairy Produce Board, Michaelis Bayley

Plastics, Dulux Australia, BHP, IOOF, Financial Synergy and Council of Adult Education.

As a buyer of print in my advertising agency days, I learned the skills and benefits of "desktop printing" which largely meant providing a personal, reliable and cost effective service underwriting and managing creative, pre-press services and supervising the final printed product sub-contracted to outside sources.

35 years later we are retired and enjoying grandchildren and the fruits of our labour.

Credits

This book is dedicated to anyone who has ever worked in a printing office.

Thanks to everyone who contributed to this book:

Mike Wilson, Roy Daniels, George Clark, Arthur Johnson, Malcolm Gregory, Albert W Perez, Graeme How, David Andrus, Dean Nayes, Thomas A Berkheiser, Alan Young, Greg Fischer, Bob Turner, Roy Bowker, Frank Granger, Dan Williams, Steve Young, Les Smith, G G Whymann, Minhinnick, George Finn and Don Hauser.

CPSIA information can be obtained
at www.ICGtesting.com
Printed in the USA
LVOW03s2034080118
562226LV00003B/572/P